PREFACE

Hello and welcome to "Confidential Caravan Buying Guide"

The first time caravanners handbook to Buying a Caravan while avoiding common expensive mistakes.

Firstly, I'd like to take this opportunity to thank you for buying my book!

Being my first publication, I am nervous (but silently confident). My goal is that by the end of the book, you will be confident enough to start making some inquiries about purchasing your first caravan. But most of all, I hope that you and your family are able to get the enjoyment that so many others do from caravanning.

CONFIDENTIAL CARAVAN BUYING GUIDE

PAUL GARROD

TABLE OF CONTENTS

About the Author

Don't worry; I'm not going to bore you with my life story. I just want to tell you a bit about my background so that you can read in confidence that I am qualified to tell you what I know. (If you don't care and just want to get to the "good stuff", feel free to skip this section – otherwise, read on...)

My name is Paul Garrod, I live in the heart of Suffolk in England, United Kingdom. My family owned a caravan and motorhome dealership for a little over 56 years. I am the grandson of the company's founder and I spent the best part of my life (about 35 years) working and running the business.

I aim to give you my professional advice to avoid expensive mistakes when buying a used touring caravan. In this book you receive my wisdom from a lifetime of experience within the caravan industry.

Things to look for which are sometimes hidden for covered up. Jargon busting explanations on terms used within the caravan market, and practical buying points to help you get the correct caravan for enjoyable holiday getaways.

As you might imagine, growing up surrounded the leisure industry was very exciting. I took every opportunity to get stuck in and learn what I could which enabled me to do my part for the family business.

Having worked in almost every department of the business (accessory shop, sales, marketing, admin, and workshop) I gathered quite a wealth of knowledge and experience that I would like to share to in order to help bring more people to the world of caravanning.

My time spent in the sales department made it very clear that there are a *lot* of questions that someone considering buying their first caravan might have – and so this book was born.

As you may already know; I also run a blog called How2Caravan.com. I help new and seasoned caravanners alike with their caravanning questions and concerns. There is lots of advice and helpful tips that will be useful if you are just starting on out on your caravanning adventure.

Throughout the book there are several paper exercises I have put together. Be sure to a pen and paper handy to follow along with them.

Now, let's get on with it!

CHAPTER 1

What Is A Caravan?

Yes, I know you know what a caravan *is*, but do you know what it can do for you? For most caravan owners, they are more than just a white box with wheels. A caravan can offer you so much; fun, freedom, enjoyment and adventure. I asked the readers of my blog to summarise caravanning in one sentence; here are some of the best ones:

> *"The best decision we ever made was to buy a caravan"*
> *– Julie from Dorset*

> *"Caravanning brings our busy family together"*
> *– Dave from Swansea*

> *"A breath of fresh air when compared to aeroplanes and competing for sunbeds"*
> *– Brian from Norwich*

> *"Fun, affordable and adored by all the family"*
> *– Sandra from Solihull*

I don't know about you, but I love statistics. I have a few industry statistics for you here courtesy of The NCC:

"The Caravan Industry in the UK:

- *Contributes more than £6billion p.a. to the UK economy (revenue from sales of products and related services, holiday bookings etc.)*

- *Employs about 130,000 people, including part time and seasonal staff (mainly on parks)*

- *Caravanning is an important contributor to UK tourism (source = VisitEngland's GBTS Annual Survey 2013)*

- *More than 51 million nights are spent in caravans each year*

In the UK, it is estimated that there are in current use:

- *550,000 touring caravans*

- *330,000 caravan holiday homes*

- *More than 205,000 motorhomes*

  = over 1 million leisure caravans."

Source: www.thencc.org/our_industry/statistics.aspx

What do you want from a caravan?

I believe that in order for you to make an informed decision and buy the right caravan, you first of all need to decide what you want the caravan to offer you. In this first chapter, I have a little fact finding mission for you that will help you to discover (if you haven't already) what sort of caravan would suit you best. Even if you have a good idea of what you want, this exercise may still prove fruitful.

One of the most wonderful things about caravans is their versatile ability to accommodate such a wide spectrum of people. Whether you're a family of 6 or there's just the 2 of you, there is caravan out there to suit you.

When I say "what do you want from a caravan" what I really mean is, what does your caravan need to be able to do for you? You need to ask yourself a few simple questions; your answers will set the base of your search for your first caravan:

1. Where do you intend to go with your caravan? Will you travel in the UK, will you venture overseas?

2 Who will be travelling with you? Will you go alone, with your partner, children, grandchildren?

3 How long will you travel for? Will you be taking short weekend trips, week long or 2 week long trips? Maybe longer?

It's time to grab your pen and notepad and begin writing the answers to the questions above as best you can. Right now it is not crucial that you are able to give 100% full answers as plans and circumstances can, and will change. You can revisit these questions at any time. Remember that there are no right or wrong answers because this is all about what suits you and your family the best.

Let's take a look at your answers...

As we already discussed, the answers to these questions will help you to get a fairly solid idea of what sort of caravans you could consider during your search.

Your answer to question 1: "Where do you intend to go with your caravan", will help you to decide how big or small your caravan needs to be and what sorts of facilities it needs to have. For example; if you are going to be travelling into Europe, could you cope on a 1,000 mile trip through France and Spain in a 12 foot caravan with no air conditioning? I know I couldn't! By considering your travel plans carefully you can quickly exclude certain caravans from your shopping list. There will be some caravans that are better suited to travelling abroad and others that are not.

Your answer to question 2; "Who will be travelling with you", can help to identify what size, berth and layout of caravan would suit your requirements. Typical caravans are 2 – 6 berth. But all of them are fitted with a rail on the side that enables you to fit an awning to it.

Awnings can soon turn a 6 berth into an 8 berth caravan, or simply offer extra living space ideal for entertaining friends of an evening.

And finally your answer to question 3, "How long will you travel for", helps you to think, practicality. Even if there are only 2 of you, is a little 2 berth caravan going to seem a bit cramped after 3 weeks? Something a little bigger might suit better. You might also decide that if you plan on taking longer trips that you would prefer a caravan with more of the "creature comforts". Alternatively, if it's just short weekend getaways you're after then a basic specification might be just the ticket.

I hope you can see that by carefully analysing your answers to the above questions, you can begin to form an idea of what your future caravan looks like.

If you haven't already, make a note of your answers because we will be using them in later on in the book.

What sorts of caravans are available?

With the ever increasing popularity of caravanning, there is more available on the market than there ever has been before. Caravans come in all different shapes, sizes, weights, colours and specification. You'd think that there was only so much you could do with a 7 foot wide box on wheels, but you'd be wrong...

Caravanning is often branded with the stereotype that it is only for retired couples, this couldn't be further from the truth. In fact, families with children represent one of the largest growth areas in the sales of caravans and have done since around 2009. The increase in demand from families has encouraged caravan manufacturers to start thinking outside of the box (no pun intended) and get more creative with the space they have to work with.

So, back to our original question; "What sorts of caravans are available?"

- **Berth** – The berth represents how many people a caravan is capable of sleeping, therefore, a 4 berth caravan is built to accommodate 4 people. You might assume that the number of berth directly correlates with the weight and length of a caravan, however, this is not always the case – but I'll talk more about that in just a moment.

- **Layout** – As the term "layout" suggests, this refers to arrangement of the furniture inside of the caravan. By those of us in the industry, the layout of a caravan is usually depicted by it's most prominent feature – for example:

  - End washroom - a dedicated washroom at the rear of the caravan

  - Fixed island bed - a permanently fixed bed that you can walk around either side of (typically located towards the rear of the caravan)

  - Fixed French bed – a permanently fixed bed positioned in the corner of the caravan

  - End lounge – long bench seats at the rear of the caravan

  - Among others...

- **Single & twin axle** – Caravans are based on both single and twin axle chassis. Caravans over 24.5 foot are usually twin axles. Both single and twin have their advantages and disadvantages. Single axles are shorter, lighter and easier to manually manoeuvre, while twin axles are sturdier on the road and offer greater living space inside but are more difficult to park and manoeuvre.

- **Size & weight** – Caravan lengths typically range anything from 10 to 26 foot. A caravan can weigh anything from

600kg – 2,500kg fully loaded, and as technology advances these weights may push as high as 3,000kg. As with berth, the length doesn't necessarily correlate to the weight of a caravan, this is usually down to the specification level.

- **Specification / model ranges** – Similar to model ranges with cars, caravans have different model tiers too which offer differing levels of specification. A common model tier structure used by caravan brands might look like this; 3 specification tiers; entry level, middle range and top of the range. Specification can have a major impact on the weight of a caravan (we'll look at why weight is important in the next chapter). You will typically find that the entry level products are mainly made up of layouts designed for families, the top of the range are predominantly layouts designed for couples while the mid range is usually a combination of the two. That being said, there are many exceptions to this.

CHAPTER 2

What Can You Tow?

Safe and legal towing disclaimer:

Information regarding towing in this chapter is intended only as a guide. I have made my best efforts to ensure that the information provided is correct at the time of writing. But please know that this is simply my interpretation.

The author or any person or company associated with the production of this book accepts no responsibility for any inaccuracies that may be in the text.

It is the responsibility of any person wishing to depend on the facts contained within this book to check for themselves with original documentation or any updating regulations, instruments or changes in the law.

Rules on these issues are likely to be changed or updated over time. Please seek further advice before you tow.

Visit: https://www.gov.uk/towing-with-car/driving-licence-rules-and-what-you-cantow for more information on safe and legal towing

Before I start baffling you with jargon I believe some definitions are in order:

Nose Weight: The weight measured at the caravan's hitch coupling when the jockey wheel is released.

MAM: Maximum Authorised Mass – This is the fully laden weight of the car complete with driver, passengers, luggage and the imposed nose weight (usually measured in kg, and is also known as MPW – Maximum Permissible Mass).

MTPLM: Maximum Technically Permissible Laden Mass – This is the fully laden weight of the caravan as stated by the manufacturer (this can be found on a plate close to the entrance door) and should not be exceeded under any circumstances. Allowances have been made for essential equipment, clothes and food (usually measured in kg).

MPTM: Maximum Permissible Towing Mass – This weight is given by the manufacturer of the car and is the maximum the vehicle is physically capable of towing (usually measured in kg).

Last one I promise...

GTW: Gross Train Weight – This is the maximum permitted combined weight of the tow car and caravan as specified by the manufacturer (usually measured in kg).

How do you find out how much a car can tow?

So, in order to ensure that the combination of the car and

caravan is a suitable match for use of the public highway you must ensure that:

- Your tow car's MAM is not exceeded

- Your caravan's MTPLM is not exceeded

- Your caravan's MTPLM does not exceed your tow car's MPTM

- The combined weight of your car's MAM and your caravan's MTPLM does not exceed your car's GTW

- The lowest load limit of these four elements is not exceeded:

  - The car's towbar and ball

  - The caravan's drawbar limit

  - The caravan's braking system overrun device

  - The caravan's hitch coupling

You will also need to make sure that the caravan's nose weight is within 5% – 7% of the actual laden weight of the caravan, this, in experience is a safe weight. So, for example, if the MTPLM of your caravan is 1500kg, your nose weight should be 75kg – 105kg (you will also need to ensure that your nose weight is less than the tow car manufacturer's nose weight recommendations).

Where can these weights can be found? There are a few places you can look:

- In your caravan's / car's handbook

- On your caravan's VIN plate (if it has one —usually found adjacent to entrance door)

- Ask the manufacturer

- Ask a dealer / caravan workshop

- Caravan Club or owners club

An easy way to go about matching your tow car against a caravan is to visit www.towsafe.co.uk where you can do an online tow match. There is a cost for this service, but it is certainly worth the money to ensure you have a safe towing outfit.

And if all that wasn't confusing enough...

Can You Tow At All?

Great! You've decided that you would like to buy a caravan; you just need to make sure that your driving license holds the correct entitlements for you to tow it.

Category B+E

A driving license with B+E entitlement allows the holder to drive vehicles up to 3,500kg MPW (Maximum Permissible Mass or MAM) and to be combined with caravans / trailers weighing in excess of 750kg MTPLM irrespective of the weight ratio. If you passed your driving test before 1st January 1997 it is likely you will have the B+E entitlement (unless it has been removed due to medical reasons).

Category B Only

A driving license with category B only allows the holder to drive vehicles up to

3,500kg MPW (with up to eight passengers including the driver) coupled with a caravan / trailer up to 750kg MTPLM (allowing a combined weight up to 4,250kg GTW). Or, a caravan over 750kg MTPLM provided the MTPLM of the caravan does not exceed the unloaded weight of the car and the combination does not exceed 3,500kg GTW.

How Do You Get B+E Entitlement?

If like me, you passed your driving test after 1st January 1997 you are not automatically given B+E entitlement. In order to get the B+E entitlement you are required to pass a further practical test.

To take the practical test you will need to get some experience with an instructor

(There are specialist instructors who can train you on this) then go ahead and take the test. I passed my test back in August 2012, I won't say it was easy but if you are willing to put in the time to practice you should be fine. The practical test is just like retaking your driving test again (that's right, you're going to need to "mirror, signal, and manoeuvre properly") but with some extra added in to ensure you are safe and able to tow too.

Useful Resources

If you would like to find out more about towing weights and license requirements then take a look at the resources below:

Towsafe - for vehicle and caravan tow matches: https://www.towsafe.co.uk **Gov UK** – more information on license entitlements etc: https://www.gov.uk/towing-withcar/driving-licence-rules-and-what-you-can-tow

CHAPTER 3

How Much Do Caravans Cost?

When buying your first caravan your budget is going to be one of the deciding factors in exactly what type of caravan you end up purchasing. That's why it's always a good idea to consider what they cost early on in your search. So what do you get for your money? In my opinion, a realistic price range of a usable caravan can range from £2,000 right up to

£30,000 (sometimes even more for hand built caravans). Here is what I think you could buy with:

- £2,000 – £4,000: This is going to buy you a very basic caravan that is likely to be 14 – 20 years old and probably starting to show it by now. You will see brands like Swift, Elddis, Compass, Abbey, Ace and Lunar (among a few others). Most will have an end dining area or large washroom as the main feature. It is unlikely that you will find many fixed beds or bunks in this price range. This price range is likely to buy you problems as far as damp and appliances are concerned unless the caravan has been well looked after by it's previous owner/s. I don't mean to put you off if this is your budget and don't get me wrong as there are plenty of very clean and tidy older caravans out there but I think it is best you be aware.

- £4,000 – £8,000: This is probably the most popular price range for second hand touring caravans. Caravans in this price range are going to be about 7 –

13 years old. If you are looking at spending this amount of money it will give you a wider selection of layouts (fixed beds were introduced in this age range). You will also find that these caravans are likely to have fewer problems and will be more reliable.

- £8,000 – £13,000: With this budget, the age of caravans you will find will generally be 3 – 6 years old. By this time the caravans have lost the largest chunk of their initial purchase price which typically happens in the first 3 years. This could work nicely in your favour as the residual value will be better over a longer period of time. A caravan of this age is likely to be quite a bit more reliable than older ones. However, it is still very important to thoroughly inspect any caravan you are looking to purchase.

- £13,000 +: If you have a budget of more than £13,000 chances are you will be looking at brand new caravans or caravans up to 2 years old. It can be a steep jump as new caravans can cost as much £30,000 for some of the top of the range models but also from as little as about £13,000. The price will very much reflect the specification of the caravan. You may be able to find some bargains where a caravan was bought new and is a year old. Someone else has already paid the VAT on it (new touring caravans are subject to VAT at the standard rate) which means big savings for you.

This leads us on nicely to...

New VS Used

As we have established previously, new caravan prices start from £13,000 which is simply not an option for some budgets. I do think it is worth at least weighing up the pros and cons of both buying a new caravan or a second hand caravan. Please note this is based on my opinion, experience and feedback from caravan owners and not by any means a complete list:

Pros of buying a new caravan:

- It's new! Nobody else has slept in your bed, used your fridge etc.

- With most new caravans, you are able to specify upholstery colour and other factory options.

- You get a long warranty from the manufacturer.

- They will be fitted with all of the latest technology.

- Only available from an authorised dealer (you get support and backup).

Cons of buying a new caravan:

- You pay a premium for new caravans.

- New caravans are subject to VAT at the standard rate making them more expensive.

- Residual value is not great for the first 3 years of ownership as this is typically when a caravan loses the largest chunk of its value.

- Not as much selection as there is when buying used.

- New caravans can be subject to teething problems. This is usually just things settling in as it is being used for the first time. These should all be rectifiable by your dealer.

Pros of buying a used caravan:

- Cheaper than buying new – you can pick your price, whatever you have to spend you should be able to find something for that price.

- Much more choice - there are thousands of used caravans on the road, you are not limited to specific layout styles that a manufacturer might decide to build for the latest models.

- When buying privately you can pick up a reasonably good deal and sometimes get accessories thrown in with the purchase (buyer beware – more on this later).

- When you buy a used caravan from a dealer it would normally come serviced and with a warranty, although you would need to confirm this with the dealer at point of purchase.

- You can often make big savings on extras already fitted that would otherwise cost thousands; motor movers, air conditioning units etc.

Cons of buying a used caravan:

- The bed will have been slept in and most, if not all of the appliances will have been used.

- Used caravans are more likely to have faults – thorough inspections are required.

- The upholstery colour cannot be changed; you are stuck with whatever scheme the person who bought it new selected.

- If you know the exact model (year, spec etc) that you are looking for it can be a challenge to find it.

Buying new or used is simply a matter of choice and or circumstance. The number one thing that leads to a used caravan purchase instead of new is budget. Having said that, many first time caravan buyers opt for second hand to "try it out" and "see if they like it" before trading up for a new one.

CHAPTER 4

Funding Your Caravan Purchase

Disclaimer: I am not a financial advisor. I have simply made a list of the most common means people use to fund the purchase of their caravan. This list does not constitute a recommendation or financial advice of any kind. Every effort has been made to ensure the correctness of this information, however, things change swiftly and information like this can become outdated very quickly. Please seek professional financial advice.

I have already spoken about how your budget is a major factor in your caravan purchase. But have you considered how you are going to pay for it yet? In my experience, people nearly always end up spending more than they had anticipated. So bare that in mind when setting your budget.

Having spent 10+ years selling caravans I witnessed the many different ways people chose to fund their caravan purchases. Below I have listed the top 6 funding sources I noticed people using:

1. Cash: Keeping it simple and paying with existing funds. "Cash" does not necessarily mean handing over pound notes;

"cash" can also represent available liquid funds.

Note: If you buy privately and are paying in hard cash please be vigilant. It is a sad thing to say, but there too many dishonest people who pray on unsuspecting buyers. At the risk of making it sound like a drug deal, I recommend that if you are paying in hard cash always take someone with you to witness the exchange. And ALWAYS remember to get a full receipt to record the transaction.

2. Hire Purchase: Most established caravan dealerships have a relationship with a specialist hire purchase financing company. The most common of these in the leisure industry is Black Horse (other names include Lombard, Barclays, Close Motor Finance among many others). A hire purchase agreement is a loan secured against the asset (in this case a caravan) where payments are made on account monthly. Ownership of the goods transfers to the buyer once the final payment has been made. Here are some of the benefits that a hire purchase agreement might offer:

-   By taking a hire purchase agreement you are entering into a tripartite agreement involving; consumer, lender and vendor. The finance company has an interested in your caravan until you make your final payment. This can be useful if you have trouble getting the dealer or manufacturer to honour the terms of the warranty.

-   A typical hire purchase agreement can last anything from 12 – 120 months (1– 10 years).

- The loan is secured against the asset (the caravan).

- You can keep your cash in the bank in case of emergencies.

3. Personal Contract Purchase (PCP) This is a form of hire purchase but instead of repaying the loan over a set amount of monthly payments a PCP is structured so that you pay a lower monthly amount over the contracted period (usually 24-48 months) leaving a final balloon payment to be made at the end of the agreement. This balloon is usually calculated to be less than the residual value of the item at the end of the contract thus allowing an equity to use as a deposit to start a new purchase.

4. Personal Loan: For people who choose to borrow money to fund their caravan purchase a personal loan is another consideration they make. The rates are often (but not always) favourable to those of hire purchase agreements. There is also a much wider range of lenders that operate in this market.

5. Equity Release: This was quite a common funding method I saw people making use of. Home owners who had equity in their property would borrow money from their mortgage provider. Similar to personal loans, these rates were often favourable.

6. Joint Purchase: I saw more and more people choosing to split the cost of a caravan purchase with friends or loved ones. More often than not it was a young family and parents. While this sounds like a great idea, be sure to consider everything

that comes with a commitment such as this. It would be rare that both parties used the caravan at the same time. It can also lead to a contrast of opinions on the size and layout of the caravan since both parties want different things from it.

7. Trade In: Trade ins / part exchanges are commonplace. During my time in the sales department I saw all sorts of things offered in as part exchange for caravans. In fact, while trading at a caravan exhibition I heard a story about a dealership who took a helicopter in as a trade in – I think that is the most obscure one I've heard of.

Second cars that spend most of their time sitting on the driveway make fantastic part exchanges. Or that motorcycle you just don't ride anymore. Most dealers will entertain anything as a trade in – just give them as much information as possible about it and they'll give you a price.

Setting your (initial) budget

A common thought among people buying their first caravan is that they don't want to spend a huge amount of money on their first purchase just in case they don't like it. Having said that, just because someone is looking to buy their first caravan it doesn't mean they haven't experienced a caravanning holiday and already knows that they are going to love it.

Which are you? Will this be your first experience holidaying in a caravan, or have you done it before?

By this time, you probably have a rough budget in mind. Make a mental note of it, because besides the purchase price of your caravan, there are additional costs you need to factor in. In the next couple of chapters I talk about those additional costs you encounter when buying and owning a caravan, plus all of the equipment required for your caravanning holidays.

CHAPTER 5

Servicing & Warranty

Caravans are made up of so many different moving and working parts. They are often referred to as a "house on wheels" because that is exactly what they are. Toilet, shower, oven, grill, hob, fridge, heater, water heater etc – all these things found within your average caravan; a box on wheels that gets dragged down the motorway at speeds in excess of 60mph. When you think of it that way, is it any surprise that things can go wrong or get broken from time to time? Regular maintenance can help to reduce the risk of faults and help to maintain a safe towing outfit. That's where servicing comes in.

As it is with a car, having your caravan serviced annually is highly recommended. Regardless of whether it is 1 year old or 20 years old. Even if it has just sat on the driveway for 12 months without moving it is equally as important. A common fault that I see in caravans that haven't been used for long periods of time is the fridge won't light on gas. The cause? 9 times out of 10 a family of spiders has made it their home and the cobwebs prevent the gas from flowing properly.

The tyres of a caravan can suffer too if it has been sitting for long period of time. It can cause your tyre to acquire a flat spot, or for the side walls to crack. This can weaken the tyre increasing the chances of a blowout.

In order to keep any outstanding manufacturer's warranty intact the caravan must be serviced on or around the anniversary of purchase. Not all service centres are approved to undertake warranty worthy service work for all brands of caravans. You may have to use an approved main dealer or an NCC Approved Workshop (to find your local NCC Approved Workshops head to www.approvedworkshops.co.uk/search). Be sure to check with the manufacturer as to their requirements – they are not all the same. This is then something you may want to consider in your budget. The cost of caravan servicing will vary from dealership to dealership but the rough average cost of a single axle caravan service is about

£225 (plus VAT, parts and sundries).

Regular servicing is not only good for maintaining the health of a caravan. It also helps for resale in the future. A good collection of service history is valued by prospective buyers and can offer them real peace of mind.

At the time of writing this, you are under no obligation to service your caravan. There is also no compulsory MOT style test for caravans either. However, you are obligated to ensure that your caravan is safe, legal and roadworthy.

You should also be aware that caravans bought under a hire purchase are required to be serviced in accordance with manufacturer's recommendations. If you do not, you stand the risk of breaching your agreement with the finance company – probably not something you want to do.

What is a caravan service and what does it include?

A caravan service is essentially a series of tests and checks that are performed to ensure the safety and integrity of a caravan. Having a caravan serviced can potentially expose some current or potential future problems which if left, could cost you a lot of money to fix and could even be potentially hazardous. Here is a brief list of some of the main things that are checked during a caravan service:

- Hitch head coupling

- Chassis

- Tyres

- Brakes

- Suspension

- Handbrake

- Road electrics

- Electrical system

- Electrical appliances

- Gas system

- Gas appliances

- Water system

- Toilet

- Bodywork

- Damp test

- And more...

Warranty

New Caravan Warranties

All new caravans come with a manufacturer's warranty. It is important you understand how these warranties are typically structured. They are often complex with some things being covered longer than others. But they can be broken down into 3 parts:

1. Body Integrity / Water Ingress: This part of the warranty guarantees against water leaking into the body of the caravan. It is commonly the longest part of the warranty; typically 5-10 years.

2. General Warranty: This part of the warranty covers the general build, fixtures and fittings and typically lasts 2-3 years.

3. Appliance Warranty: This is where things can get a little

complicated. Not all manufacturers operate the same way. Most in fact change their cover every year. The most common way for the appliances fitted within the caravan to be covered is by *their* respective manufacturers. Although you might have bought a Swift caravan, it doesn't mean they made the cooker. Depending upon who built the caravan, the warranty can be held with the appliance manufacturer directly or with the caravan manufacturer. Appliance warranties are generally 1-3 years long.

Some caravan manufacturers will offer to extend the warranty for an additional cost. These warranties can prove to be really great value for money. But be aware that most are non-transferable, meaning that if you sell the caravan the extension is voided. So unless you intend on keeping the caravan for the full term of the extension of the warranty I wouldn't waste your money on these.

Be sure to study the terms of the warranty on offer with a new caravan. As you enter the later years of the warranty less and less things are included. Some warranties can be voided if you live in your caravan, or spend more than 6 months a year abroad in it. Remember we spoke about service requirements for warranties earlier in the chapter? This is a must if you wish to keep your warranty intact. There is usually a window either side of the caravan's anniversary of purchase in which to get the caravan serviced in accordance with the terms of the warranty. This window however gets smaller as the years go by.

Oh, and in case you were wondering - self servicing your caravan is not in accordance with the terms of a new caravan's warranty.

I touched on this earlier on, but I want to help you to manage your expectations with a new caravan. After you pick it up you will be itching to get packed up and go out on your first caravan adventure in your new caravan. I recommend going somewhere not too far from home on your first trip in the caravan. Please don't take this as me knocking the build quality of caravans because I am not. It is just the reality that comes with using a product like this for the first time.

The journey your new caravan has taken since it was finished being built on the production line is quite lengthy. It will have undergone a series of tests and inspections by both the manufacturer and by the dealer before you take delivery. The thing is, you will be the first to actually live in it. So, although the shower has been tested, no one has actually taken a shower in it, although the grill has been tested, no one has actually made a bacon sarnie with it. See where I am going with this?

On your first trip away, take a notepad and paper make a list of things that didn't quite work right or things that require adjustments. Upon your return, arrange a convenient time with your dealer to return the caravan to have any of these issues rectified. This is a normal practice when buying a new car. You return it after the first 500-1,000 miles for a mini service.

Used Caravan Warranties

Warranties When Buying From A Dealership

If you buy a used caravan from a dealership chances are that it will come with a warranty of some description. If a warranty is not offered with a caravan, it could simply be down to the age of the caravan or because of a stated outstanding problem that will not be fixed by the dealer before the sale. In some circumstances it is not financially viable for a dealer to pay their technicians to repair a caravan. This is known as sold as seen.

The way one dealership manages their warranty may be different to how another does. But generally it will be an in-house warranty (one funded by the dealership themselves) or a third party, insurance backed warranty (funded by a third party insurance company). Both should offer similar coverage, but if it is an in-house warranty be sure to get a written confirmation of the cover and its exclusions.

In order for a dealer to offer a third party warranty, the caravan will have to undergone a recent service.

If the caravan is only a year or two old it may still have an outstanding manufacturer's warranty. It would need to have an up to date service record in accordance with the terms of the warranty. It would also need to be transferable – it is not common, but some manufacturers may not allow warranties to be transferred to new owners. Have the dealer check to see if there is indeed an outstanding warranty and if it can be transferred to you.

If the warranty *is* transferable, you may find that there is an administration fee payable by you to the manufacture to administer the transfer. This is usually around £15-£30, but I would say it's worth every penny of that.

Similar to how a manufacturer might offer a purchasable extended warranty, your dealer may too offer you the option to extend your warranty for a fee.

Warranties When Buying Privately

Obviously Jeff who sells you his caravan through eBay doesn't have the ability to offer a warranty with his caravan. But that doesn't mean to say you can't get a warranty for your privately purchased caravan. There are companies that specialise in these types of warranties. But they will likely require you to have the caravan serviced before you take it out.

Regardless of the fact that you bought your caravan privately – I would recommend talking to your local dealer to see if they can sell you a warranty. That way, at least you have a point of contact if ever you need to make a claim.

What Is Covered Under Warranties

It would be impossible for me to write a list of all of the things that a warranty might cover. And if I did write it, If you are not already asleep from all of this boring warranty talk, you certainly would be by the time you had finished reading it. So, instead I have compiled a shortlist of the things that most warranties have in common regarding what is covered: *Disclaimer: this list is for information purposes only, please check with the warranty provider to confirm what is covered and what is not*

- Chassis

- Suspension

- Axles

- Braking system

- Towing mechanism

- Electrical

- Water

- Gas system

- Heating system

- Cooker

- Fridge

- Cassette toilet

- Water ingress (body leaks)

- And more...

It is important to remember that wear and tear items (such as brakes and tyres etc) will not be covered under warranty. Accidental damage is also not covered. As much as it hurts your ego and your wallet; if you break something, own up and pay for it to get fixed. Don't try and pass it off as a fault – these false and fraudulent claims cost the industry hundreds of thousands of pounds every year and will only end up driving the price of everything upwards anyway.

CHAPTER 6

Caravan Insurance

Disclaimer: The information in this chapter is intended purely as a guide. It is your responsibility to do your own research and to make your own informed decision.

Top tip: Compare quotes from multiple insurance providers at www.GetCaravanQuotes.com

I promise it will save you bucket loads of time and some money too.

Whilst it isn't a legal requirement to insure you touring caravan (at least it wasn't at the time this book was published) I still believe you should definitely do it. Having said that; if you buy a caravan on a hire purchase agreement, part of your responsibility is to insure it for the full value. The finance company insist on it so that if it is damaged or stolen they will still get paid - fair enough, right?

Around 2,000 touring caravans are stolen every year in the UK! That is a rather frightening figure – and with more caravans on the road every year that number is sure to rise.

Depending on the level of cover you choose, the insurance policy will safeguard you against theft and damage.

Some of the most popular caravan insurance cover is the "new for old" policies. These offer a variation of "if your caravan is stolen or written off we will replace it with the same or similar new model".

My Car Insurance Will Cover It… Won't It?

Sorry, this is not the case. Your car insurance is cover for your car and or other vehicles you might be involved with in a road traffic accident. In fact, your existing car insurance policy may not even cover you whilst towing. Meaning that by towing a caravan you could even void your car insurance. Be sure to contact your tow car insurer and find out what cover, if any, your current policy offers whilst towing.

You may find that your tow car insurer will only cover you for towing a caravan up to a certain weight or length. Adjust your policy according to the caravan you buy to ensure you are fully covered. Remember that it is your responsibility to ensure that you are safe and legal.

How Much Does Caravan Insurance Cost?

According to CETA, the average annual caravan insurance premium is £174. From what I have seen my customers pay this sounds pretty spot on. But your premium could be affected by a number of different things. I have seen someone pay as little as £100, and another as much as £600 for their insurance. The upper scale of the price range is not particularly common but it does happen.

How To Reduce Your Insurance Premium

The formula used to generate your caravan insurance premium can vary from lender to lender. It is impossible to know exactly how they arrive at the final figure they quote to you, but there are some things you can do to qualify for discounts therefore reducing your premium. I have made a list of things I have know to reduce caravan insurance premiums. Remember that not all of these will apply to every insurance company.

Fitted caravan security features – some insurance companies will offer discounts if you have any of the following security accessories fitted to your caravan:

- Tracking system

- Alarm

- Electronic trailer stability system

- Lockable corner steadies

- Security door handle

Removable caravan security accessories – some insurers will offer discounts if you have some of the following removable caravan security accessories:

- Hitch lock

- Wheel lock

- Corner steady locks

Club memberships – being a member of a club can bring discounts from certain insurers:

- The Caravan Club

- The Camping & Caravanning Club

Storage Location Matters

Your caravan's storage location is an important thing to consider. Not only can storing in certain places reduce your premium, but can also minimise the security risk to your caravan giving you peace of mind. Here are some the places I have known people to store their caravans:

- On the driveway

- On site (permanently pitched)

- In a farmer's barn (this tends to scare insurance companies resulting in potentially higher premiums)

- CaSSOA secure storage site

There is one storage location from the list that I want to talk more about; CaSSOA (Caravan Storage Site Owners' Association). CaSSOA is an organisation that was formed in 1999 to help combat caravan theft. In order for a storage location to be eligible for a CaSSOA accreditation they have to go through an on site survey. The site earns points for various security features that they have (such as full perimeter fencing, lockable gates, CCTV, monitored entry and exit among others) and are awarded either; Bronze, Silver or Gold accreditation with Gold level being the highest.

Here are the security features you can expect to see at each accreditation level for CaSSOA sites:

Bronze: Perimeter protection and locked gates.

Silver: Bronze security features plus CCTV & monitored entry and exit.

Gold: Bronze and Silver security features plus access control and alarms.

You will typically find that the cost of storing at a CaSSOA site is according to its level of accreditation; Bronze is the cheapest, followed by Silver, and Gold being the most expensive.

Comparing all of the storage options in my list, storing at a CaSSOA registered site is most likely to give you a discount on your insurance premium. The discount tier that most insurance companies adopt is also relative to the level of accreditation the site has been awarded resulting in the largest discounts being given for storing at Gold sites.

Some interesting statistics were revealed by a government study; nearly 50% of caravan thefts are carried out on caravans stored in private driveways, around 45% of caravans are stolen from service stations and holiday sites while only 5% are stolen from caravan storage sites. Need I say any more?

Holidaying Abroad Can Affect Your Premium Too

One of the questions most insurance companies ask you is "do you plan on travelling overseas?". If your answer is yes, then expect to pay a little bit more for your insurance. For insurance companies, you're travelling overseas represents an increased risk to the caravan which causes an increase in premium. We're not talking big bucks really, but it is worth mentioning all the same.

I have seen some insurance companies including overseas cover complete with roadside assistance.

If the insurance company does not ask about overseas travel and you do plan on doing so, be sure to confirm whether it is included in your cover or not.

Shopping Around Can Save You Money

Do I really need to tell you this? Probably not – but you would be surprised how many people just go with the first insurance company they find without seeing if they can get a better deal elsewhere. I do understand why though, it can be time consuming to call 4-5 different companies or fill in multiple online forms to get a quote.

I have found that the easiest way to shop around if to let someone else do the legwork for you. I found a website that will find the best deal for you. All you have to do is fill in a simple form on their website and that's it! They will then do what they do best and contact you with the best quote they could find. Here is the website if you want to give it a try www.getcaravanquotes.com

Never Accept The Renewal Price

Accepting the renewal price on your caravan could also prove a costly mistake to make. Towards the end of your policy the insurance company will write to you with a renewal quote. More often than not it will be substantially more expensive than it was for the year before.

Make use of a service like www.getcaravanquotes.com again to search out the best deal for you.

CHAPTER 7

Caravanning Equipment

E ven though caravans are fitted out with plenty of home from home, there are still certain pieces of equipment that you will need to enjoy your caravanning holidays in comfort. I have compiled a list of what I believe to be the bare necessities of additional equipment along with a description of its purpose and a rough estimation of the cost of each. Depending upon your style of touring, you may not *need* everything, but the list is what 99% of caravanners use:

- **Fresh Water Carrier** – The fresh water that is fed to your kitchen and bathroom sinks and your shower is supplied by the fresh water carrier. It is usually in the form of a cylinder with a handle that connects on the top and base of the carrier so that it can be rolled along for ease of transport from the site's fill point.

Some of the most popular fresh water carriers available on the market are called "Aquaroll" and "Water Hog". There are 2 different sizes – I would recommend the larger. You will be surprised how quickly you use your fresh water. A larger container reduces the frequency of your visit to the fill point.

Approximate cost = £40.00 – £60.00

- **Waste Water Carrier** – The waste water (or grey water as it is also known) collected from the drains of the kitchen and bathroom sink and shower is stored in the waste water carrier.

Waste water carriers are usually fitted with a handle and wheels to make transport to the waste water point easy. The typical storage capacity of a waste carrier is around 45-50 litres. Two examples of popular waste water carriers are "Wastemaster" and "Waste Hog".

Approximate cost = £40.00 – £60.00

- **12V Leisure Battery** – Touring caravans make use of three different power sources. 12V is largely responsible for running low power appliances and equipment "under the hood".

With a 12V battery fitted you can tour standalone for a period of time without the need to connect to mains. Note that the period of time can vary drastically based on the charge and usage of the battery.

A regular 12V car battery is not suitable for use in caravans. Leisure batteries have been specifically designed for the infrequent use that is common with caravans (car batteries are used on a daily basis).

Leisure batteries for caravans typically come in a variation of two sizes; 85ah and 110ah. For larger caravans, those that will go without mains power for extended periods and those that have caravan movers fitted it is recommended to use the larger 110AH battery. Otherwise an 85ah will be sufficient.

Approximate cost = £60.00 – 140.00

- **Gas Bottle** – Gas is another power source utilised by touring caravans. It is responsible for powering things like your; fridge, water heater and heating system.

Most caravans accommodate 2 cylinders which are usually stowed in the front locker. Some designs saw the "gas locker" feature on the side of the caravan.

There are two types of gas that can be used; Butane and Propane. Both are readily available nationally and internationally. But they do have some differences that make Propane the better choice. Propane is; lighter, cheaper, burns hotter and does not freeze in the winter.

All of these points make it a better choice over Butane gas. Calor Gas (who are the biggest supplier of the cylinders used in caravans) developed an aluminium gas cylinder specifically designed for use within touring caravans. It contains 6kg of gas, and the cylinder weighs an impressive 49.7% less than the standard steel cylinder, thus reducing the nose weight of your caravan.

Approximate cost = In excess of £70 (per cylinder) if you do not already own a cylinder

- **Mains Lead** – Mains electric is the main power source for caravans. It is responsible for powering; fridge, water heater, heating, lighting and freestanding appliances such as televisions and radio

The mains lead connects to the mains point on the site to supply caravan 240V power.

Mains leads come in many different lengths from 10 – 25m. I would recommend getting the longest one you can find since it is always better to have too much cable than not enough.

The mains cable needs to be of suitable requirements and those include the thickness of the cores of the cable (2.5mm), the colour of the outer shell must be orange and it must 1 plug and one socket, both waterproof.

You can buy these from any caravan accessory shop. Approximate cost = £15.00 - £30.00

- **Step** – The entrance into a caravan is roughly a 1 – 2 foot from the ground. Having a step is a must to ensure safe access to the caravan.

You can buy all sorts of different types; single steps, double steps, steps with hand rails and all made from either plastic or metal.

If you are not confident on foot, I would recommend

getting a rubber topped step. Plastic and metal topped steps can get quite slippery in the wet.

If you buy a new caravan, most will include a basic plastic single step from the factory.

Approximate cost = £15.00 – £30.00

- **Hitch Lock** – As discussed in the previous chapter, ensuring the security of your caravan is very important. Hitch locks are designed to prevent thieves from hitching up to your caravan.

There are lots of different hitch locks to choose from. Look out for the ones with the "Sold Secure" logo featured on the packaging. Sold Secure hitch locks are usually approved by caravan insurance companies.

Most touring caravans are built on an AL-KO chassis and so require a hitch lock suitable for the AL-KO hitch head. While a small number of brands; Elddis, Compass, Buccaneer and Xplore are built on the BPW chassis which also requires a specific type of hitch lock – be sure to check which type you need before purchasing.

Some hitch locks are considered to be better than others. The "better" ones bring with them increased security and in some cases increased discounts on your caravan insurance premium too.

Approximate cost of hitch lock = £70 – £120

- **Wheel Lock** – A wheel lock in addition to a hitch lock adds yet more security and peace of mind. Insurance approved models also feature the "Sold Secure" logo.

Depending upon A; whether your wheel is steel or alloy, and B; whether you have the AL-KO Secure Wheel Lock Receiver on your chassis will determine the type of wheel lock you have to choose from.

There are *so many* different types of caravan wheel locks on the market. Some fit only steel wheels, others only alloy wheels. Later caravans with alloy wheels built on the AL-KO chassis were fitted with the AL-KO Secure Wheel Lock Receiver.

The AL-KO secure wheel lock is by far the most expensive lock. It is also arguably the best lock on the market and is preferred by most insurers. The lock itself is a small solid metal lozenge that fits in between the spokes of the wheel and locks into the receiver on the chassis.

Approximate cost = £50 - £300

- **Corner Steady Handle** – All corners of a caravan are fitted with a corner steady. The steadies are lowered to maintain the level and stability of the caravan while pitched up on site.

To raise and lower the corner steadies you need a tool called a corner steady handle. The handle fits around the bolt in the corner steady and is wound clockwise and anticlockwise and clockwise to raise and lower the steadies.

There is an alternative to the traditional manual corner steady handle – you can now buy a corner steady jack drill bit which takes seconds to wind the legs up and down.

If you buy a new caravan, most will include a corner steady handle from the factory. Approximate cost = £10.00 - £20.00

- **Water Pump** – The water pump attaches to water inlet on the outside of the caravan and drops into the fresh water carrier feeding the water to the taps as required.

There are many different types of water pumps. Your caravan will require a specific type which will be determined by the age and brand of the caravan and which water system is fitted. Be sure to check with a dealership or manufacturer which one your caravan needs.

Because they pumps are caravan specific, they tend to change hands with the caravans when they are sold. You should only really need to buy one if yours is faulty or missing. They are also supplied with factory fresh caravans.

Approximate cost £30.00 – £70.00

- **Toilet Chemicals** – Unless you buy an older, more basic model of caravan, it will come fitted with a chemical toilet. As its name suggests, a chemical toilet uses chemicals.

There are two types of chemicals that are used; blue and pink. The blue chemical is used in the cassette of the toilet to break down solid waste, and the pink goes into the flush.

A couple of popular brands of toilet chemical are "Elsan" and "Thetford".

It is important to use the chemicals because they keep the toilet clean, sanitary and help to combat unpleasant odours.

Approximate cost = £10.00 - £15.00 per bottle

- **Spirit Level** – A small and seemingly insignificant accessory, but boy do you need one.

A spirit level serves only one purpose but solves multiple potential problems. Having a spirit level ensures that the caravan is horizontally level on the ground. If the caravan is not level it could; prevent the fridge from working on gas, put unnecessary stress on one or two of the corner steadies and make for a very uncomfortable night sleep.

Approximate cost = £2.00 – £5.00

- **Nose Weight Gauge** – I talked about the importance of knowing your nose weight in Chapter 2. I want to reinforce it again – you need to ensure that your nose weight is within the recommended limit given by your tow car's manufacturer. If your nose weight is over the recommended limit it could potentially be dangerous to you and other road users.

Not surprisingly, nose weight gauges are used to measure the nose weight of your caravan. You should take the nose weight in the condition you expect to tow the caravan, i.e. fully laden.

The nose weight gauge is placed under the hitch head of

the caravan whilst the jockey wheel is lowered. The nose weight gauge then takes the weight of the front of the caravan at which point you take the measurement before re-securing the jockey wheel and removing the nose weight gauge.

You can also buy digital nose weight gauges, but they are considerably more expensive and not really necessary in my opinion.

Approximate cost = £10.00 – £50.00

- Some of the above items can be purchased from my online shop www.how2caravan.com/shop

CHAPTER 8

Caravan Clubs & Organisations

One of the most exciting things about caravanning is getting involved with the many clubs. It is a pretty lively scene with a rally, meet-up, party or something going on near enough every week. If you are not a part of it then you're missing out.

There are two main types of club in the caravan industry; the smaller member run clubs and the larger organisation clubs. The member run clubs are usually Owner's Clubs that are specifically for owners of a certain brand of caravan. The larger clubs are corporate authority organisations formed to give support and advice to their members.

The Caravan and Motorhome Club (the largest club in the industry) also has smaller local subsidiaries of the club known as "Centres". The Centres are generally member run and operate semi-independently to the main club.

The smaller clubs are generally non-profits that enable like minded people to come together and have a great time.

There are easily more than 100 different clubs to choose from, but here is a small sample list of some popular ones:

- The Caravan and Motorhome Club – Previously known as "The Caravan Club". It is the longest standing and largest club with nearly 1 million members and most respected club in the industry

- The Camping & Caravanning Club – The oldest club for all forms of camping and has over 500,000 members

- The Compass Club – Compass caravan owners club

- Burstner Club – Burstner caravan owners club

- The Bailey Owners' Caravan Club – Bailey caravan owners club

- Lunar Owners Club – Lunar caravan owners club

- Buccaneer Owners Club – Buccaneer caravan owners club

- The Swift Owners' Club – Swift caravan owners club

- The AAOCC (All Avondale Owners' Caravan Club) – Avondale caravan owners club

- The Elddis Owners Club – Elddis caravan owners club

- Bessacarr Owners Club – Bessacarr caravan owners club

- The ABI & Friends Caravan Club – ABI caravan owners club

- Abbey Caravan Owners Club – Abbey caravan owners club

- Sterling Caravan Owners Club – Sterling caravan owners club

There are, of course, many other clubs. Be sure to take a good look around for a club to join -- you can enjoy some fantastic perks and benefits simply by being a member of certain clubs.

What To Expect From The Clubs

Each club has its own unique offerings. To put them all into the same basket would be a mistake. There is so much more that can be gained from joining a club than I can put into words, but here is a list of just some of things you might expect from a club:

- Expert advice

- Form new friendships with like minded people

- Become a part of a strong community

- Discounts from supporting dealers

- Discounts from supporting insurance companies

- Access to "member only" sites

- Preferential pricing and access at certain sites

- Print material such as site guides, magazines and more

- Access to join local Centres

- Invitation to "member only" rallies

The one thing that *all* of the clubs have in common is the social aspect. Every one of them welcomes new members with open arms and are keen to forge relationships that will last a life time.

The NCC – National Caravan Council

The NCC was formed in 1939 as the UK trade body representing the collective interests of the tourer, motorhome, holiday home and park home sectors.

The NCC is simply a club for the industries manufacturers, traders and retailers. Although you, the consumer cannot become a member, it is certainly worth knowing they are and what they do.

The two biggest caravan and motorhome shows of the year are held at Birmingham's National Exhibition Centre – one in February and the other in October. The NCC is responsible for the organisation and running of these two shows.

There are certain industry-wide standards that manufacturers, dealers and service & repair workshops are expected to adhere to. The NCC is also responsible governing these expectations and ensuring that they are fulfilled.

You may have heard of "The Approved Workshop Scheme". Service and repair workshops receive the "NCC Approved Workshop" accreditation so long as they work to a certain standard of safety and quality. I would always recommend using these workshops as you can be sure of the level of workmanship. If you receive less than satisfactory work you can contact The NCC who can help to resolve the issue.

Should You Join A Club?

Should you join a club? I recommend you do, especially if you are just getting started in the caravan world. Even after reading this book you will still have lots of questions – if you are a part of a club there is always someone to turn to.

I always recommend everyone to join The Caravan and Motorhome Club. There is so much the club has to offer you. If you are interested in joining go to www.joincaravanclub.com where you can submit your application in just a few minutes online.

CHAPTER 9

Who & Where To Buy From

Once you have decided the type of caravan you would like and what your budget is, it is time to start thinking about where you are going to buy it from.

A common dilemma caravan buyers struggle with is whether to buy privately or from a dealership. Naturally both come with their advantages and disadvantages. But which one are you most comfortable with?

Advantages Of Buying Privately

- Cheaper – you are likely to pay less for a caravan when buying it privately.

- Comes with accessories – some people choose to sell their caravans complete with all the accessories; this can help to save quite a bit of money.

- You may know the owner and therefore the history of the caravan.

Disadvantages Of Buying Privately

- Sold as seen – there is no backup or warranty from a private seller.

- It is unlikely the seller has had the caravan fully checked over for faults before they sell it.

- No real legal comeback if something goes wrong or a hidden fault appears – buyer beware.

- You are restricted to a few different payment options; debit / credit card and hire purchase are not an option.

- Handing over large sums of cash can be dangerous – always take someone with you when buying cash.

Advantages Of Buying From A Dealership

- Buying from a dealership means your purchase comes with a warranty (unless otherwise stated)

- You have access to a wealth of backup, support and advice in the dealership.

- Dealerships have certain obligations to the sale of a caravan

- Browsing at dealerships is much easier because you can view lots of caravans in one place.

- There are multiple payment options including credit and debit card, and if the dealership has the facility you may be able to apply for hire purchase.

Disadvantages Of Buying From A Dealership

- More expensive – the standard preparation process of a caravan purchased from a dealer includes; pre-delivery inspection / service and full valet. This peace of mind comes with an additional cost.

- Accessories come at an additional cost.

This is by no means a full and complete list, I am sure you could add a few of your own to the list.

Whether you decide to buy privately or from a dealership is entirely up to you – there is no right and wrong to it, but you don't need me to tell you that. Make a decision based on what you know and what best suits your individual circumstances.

Finding Caravans For Sale

When you are looking to buy a caravan there are many different places you can find them advertised for sale. Here is a quick list of the places you will find caravans for sale:

- www.CaravanFinder.co.uk – Caravan Finder is one of the largest platforms for people looking to both buy and sell caravans. There are thousands of new and used caravans for sale from dealerships and private sellers alike.

- You can even select a specific layout and search the website that way – perfect if you know the exact layout you are looking for.

- www.CaravansForSale.co.uk – Caravans For Sale is another

huge website cataloguing thousands of caravans for sale from dealerships and private sellers.

- **www.AutoTrader.co.uk/caravans** – Auto Trader have a section on their website specifically for touring caravans.

- **www.Ebay.co.uk** – On eBay you can snag incredible bargains when you buy caravans at auction. But you will also find classified ads for both new and used caravans from dealerships and private sellers.

- **www.Preloved.co.uk** – Preloved is not a largely known website but I have found it to be somewhat of a gem when hunting for caravans. There are some fantastic bargains to be had. Sellers include both dealerships and private individuals.

- **www.Gumtree.co.uk** – Gumtree is a classified ad site owned by eBay. Most of the caravans for sale on Gumtree are from private sellers.

- **Dealer websites** – Caravan dealerships tend to have their full inventory of caravan stock on their websites. Expect to find detailed descriptions and specifications.

- **Magazines** – Some of the major magazines include a private classified ad section at the end. I have noticed there are quite a few "bundle" sales that include all the accessories with the sale of the caravan.

- **Local Paper** – You may even find private classified ads for caravans in the back of your local paper. My local paper has a weekly "Motors Feature" that includes adverts for caravans too.

- **Notice Boards** – Good old fashioned notice board adverts are still around and often offer bargain deals. You can find these in public libraries, post offices, caravan sites, churches, etc.

- **Local Dealership** – Take a trip down to your local dealership and browse their display of caravans at your leisure.

Beware The Scams

Buying a caravan is a very exciting time for anyone. After all, you are on the search for the vehicle that will take you on lots of incredible adventures! This excitement is often what blinds us from what would otherwise seem obvious – the scams.

Having grown up in the caravan world I have heard my fair share of horror stories. Every story had one thing in common – the deal was too good to be true. Every time someone was lured in by a scam. It all began with an advert for a caravan that was ridiculously cheap. So cheap that you might look at the ad and think "they've obviously made a typo on their price".

If a deal looks too good to be true it probably is.

Some other telltale signs and tricks used by scammers include:

- Urgency on sending a deposit via bank transfer or PayPal. They will probably tell you they have others waiting to buy if you don't. Never transfer any money without physically seeing the caravan.

- They are always "out of the country".

- The English (spelling, punctuation and grammar) is often pretty awful.

- They usually include a "God bless you" or similar religious saying to attempt to convince you of their innocence and supposed good nature.

- Need you to wire funds to their "friend" via MoneyGram or Western Union.

- They avoid letting you arrange to physically view goods.

If any correspondence you are having with a seller looks anything like this list then immediately cease all communications. It is *highly* likely that it is a scam – it is always better to be safe than sorry.

CHAPTER 10

What To Look Out For When Buying A Caravan

I said it in the previous chapter, buying a caravan is an extremely exciting time. But when you are looking around a caravan with the mind to purchase it you need to put the excitement to one side and engage the rational part of your brain.

Caravans are wonderful creations – they are fitted out pretty much everything we need to live comfortably. But unfortunately that means that things can, and will go wrong. It is wise to perform your due diligence before you buy so to avoid any potential nasty surprises further down the line.

I recommend going on a fact find mission with each caravan you view which should help to paint a better picture of the current state of the caravan, how well the previous owners have looked after it and if there are likely to be any problems in the near future.

Please do bear in mind that although you may have carefully checked everything and that your fact finding revealed nothing of any concern, things can still go wrong at any time for no apparent reason. It only takes one trip down road for a wire to shake loose and one of the lights to stop working – I use this as an example to illustrate my point.

Check For Service History

Just like your car does, caravans have a service book. The book should be stamped by the servicing workshop each and every time a service is carried out. Keeping good records such as this could help future technicians to understand what work has been carried out and when on the caravan in the past (this can help you save money on diagnostic time).

Unfortunately it is quite common for service books not to be stamped. Instead, you may find printouts of service records. The printed service records do offer more detail on outstanding issues and recommendations for future work.

A full service history gives you a window into how well the caravan has been cared for by its previous owners. A caravan lacking a history may suggest that it has not been well cared for which might raise a red flag for you.

Service history can get lost – in this case you could ask the seller where they have had their work carried out. You could then contact the workshop and request confirmation that the work has been carried out and get copies of the records.

Has The Caravan Undergone Past Repairs?

There are a couple of reasons you need to know if the caravan has previously undergone any kind of repairs. If it has:

1. Did the repair come with a guarantee that is still valid? If the repair is recent and it fails you need to know if you can take it back to where it was repaired to be out right.

2. Was the repair for a known fault? Some caravans have known faults that once resolved, shouldn't be problematic again. Knowing that these have been fixed can give you peace of mind.

Another type of repair to look out for is the larger repair carried out as a the result of an insurance claim. Caravans are not recorded as "write offs" on their keeper certificates. If such repairs *have* been carried out you want to know by whom and if and how long the work is guaranteed for. Poor workmanship on large scale repairs can affect the integrity of the caravan.

Check For Outstanding Finance

I talked about hire purchase in Chapter 4. The loan is secured against the asset and title of the goods does not transfer until the final payment has been made. For someone to attempt to sell a caravan that they do not have good title to is extremely wrong and in breach of their hire purchase agreement.

If the caravan has outstanding finance on it and you still wish to buy it ensure that the seller clears the finance *before* you give them any money. Do not trust that they will pay it off when you leave. If they do not clear the finance and they stop making payments then the finance company is within their rights to reclaim their asset, leaving you with no money and no caravan.

Fortunately there is a quick and easy way to find out if a caravan still has finance on it. Go to www.cris.co.uk/cris-check where you can perform a CRiS Check online. It will also tell you:

- If the caravan has been reported stolen

- If the caravan has been previously written off by insurance companies

- The details of the registered keeper

A CRiS check costs around £15.00 which, in my opinion, is worth every penny.

Check For Damp

Damp is probably the most feared problem with a caravan. The trouble with damp is that once it has truly set in, it can be extremely costly to rectify it. Even if you are able to fix it, chances are that the caravan will never be as it once was.

Damp could be compared to a serious human disease; if diagnosed early, treatment can be given and a full recovery is much more likely.

It is important that you are able to spot both the early warning signs of a potential damp problem and those of a serious one.

Though damp is more common in older caravans, it doesn't mean that a 3 year old caravan cannot be affected. Water can find its way into a caravan in many different ways. A small pin prick sized hole on the roof could, over time, cause a serious damp problem in the ceiling. Or, damage to an awning rail could rupture the seal and allow water to slowly creep in.

Be sure to give a thorough inspection of the outside of the caravan noting any damage that could potentially allow water to penetrate the outer skin.

I mentioned earlier that there are telltale signs that can occur with damp. Here is a list of some of the most common ones:

- **Smell** – The smell of a caravan is the first tell-tale sign I notice when walking into a caravan. Mouldy smells often indicate there may be some damp which by this stage is normally quite extensive. Also take note of any pleasant overpowering smells that may have been planted in the caravan to cover the damp smell.

- **Dark Patches** – Dark patches on the wall board under and around windows, in the corners where the wallboard joins, along ceiling joints and the wall board of the washroom can indicate that water has penetrated it. The dark spots are not easy to spot in bad lighting – I recommend taking a torch.

- **Spongy Walls** – The wall board of a caravan should be solid. If it is spongy then the caravan is suffering from a severe damp problem.

- **Black Wood** – Carefully lift the black rubber that surrounds the inside of a window aperture. The wood should be a normal colour. If it is black and slimy this is an indication that there is water coming in somewhere around the window.

- **Flaky Wall Board** – Crispy, flaky wall board is a sign of an old damp problem that may have dried out on its own. That doesn't mean that there is nothing to worry about

  – it requires further inspection.

- **Pimply Wall Board** – Wall board should be smooth (besides those with a raised pattern on them). Small prickly pimples indicate that water could be coming in behind the wall board.

- **Different Wall Board** – A common trick used to cover up an existing damp problem is to "board over". It usually stands out like a sore thumb because the wall board does not match. In some cases a board over job is okay – but be sure to look into it further.

To perform a thorough damp inspection you are going to need a damp meter. Using a damp meter will help you to determine how serious the damp problem is without the guesswork.

You can buy a good damp meter for around £25.00 which is money well spent considering the trouble it could save you from buying into

To get yours go to www.how2caravan.com/shop. while stocks last.

A damp meter gives you readings as a percentage. You need to be able to interpret those percentages and decide whether the caravan is damp or not. Here is how I interpret the percentages from my damp meter:

- 0 – 20% – normal readings = no problem

- 20 – 25% – higher than average = further inspection required

- 30% + – high damp readings = damp problem

To obtain these readings, the prongs of the damp meter need to be gently poked into the wall board. Here is a list of all the places I recommend checking for damp with your meter:

- Under windows – check around the corners of the windows and lift the rubber to make sure the stick work is not black and sticky.

- Around the entrance door.

- Around the outer aperture of any external lockers, mains and gas BBQ points

- Front and rear corners of the caravan where the wall board joins.

- In the top storage lockers where the side panel meets the roof.

- Around the outside of roof lights.

- Side panel joins – If the caravan's side panels consist of two joining pieces of metal, try to check along the join on the inside of the caravan.

- Along the edges of the floor where the floor joins the sides of the caravan.

NOTE: Inserting the damp meters prongs into rubber seals or against metal will give a false reading that does not reflect water content, do not be confused by this. Only insert prongs into wood / wall board.

Some later caravans including Bailey and Swift so not use wooden wall board – It has been replaced with GRP. Do not attempt to insert damp meter prongs into the GRP.

Miscellaneous, Costly To Repair Problems

There are a few other main things I look for when inspecting a caravan. These are problems that can be quite expensive to put right:

- **Spongy Floor** – A soft, springy, spongy floor means that the caravan is suffering from "delamination". Delamination tends to occur in older caravans and is the result of many years of people walking up and down.

  Delaminated floors can be repaired – this is done by drilling a hole in the floor and injecting a solution into the floor. The solution hardens and reduces the sponginess of the floor.

  The job involves carefully cutting the carpet or lino flooring – if this is not done neatly you will always be able to see the scars.

- **Blown / Cracked Windows** – Caravan windows are double glazed and sealed. If the seal between the panes is compromised and air is allowed to get in between the double glazing it can cause them to swell (hence a blown window). The swelling of the window can pull the window away from the seals allowing water to get in.

Similarly, cracked windows compromise the water-tightness of the caravan. Blown windows can be repaired, but it is only temporary. They will otherwise need replacing.

The cost of a replacement window starts at around £250. Some of the larger windows can cost in excess of £800 to replace.

- **Cracked Sinks & Shower Trays** – It is quite common to find a cracked sink or shower tray. Some of the earlier models become brittle over time – it only takes a heavy bottle of shampoo to be dropped in the shower to crack it.

A crack in the shower could allow water to get into the floor of the caravan. Complete replacement of a shower tray is not always necessary. There is a repair that consists of a liquid plastic solution being sprayed over the base of the shower tray – it is then left to set and harden. Once hard the shower tray is secure once again.

Cracked sinks however will likely need to be replaced. The costs vary considerably depending upon the size and material.

- **Split Shower Heads & Taps** – Splits in shower heads and taps can be a telltale sign of a much more serious problem – frost damage. Damage like this means that the caravan was not properly winterised.

If water is left in the system over the winter period it will freeze, expand and cause extensive damage to tanks, pipes and taps.

- **Damaged Work Surfaces** – Caravan work surfaces are designed and built to be light weight. They are made up using a honeycomb type inside to provide strength to the surface. However, a tin of beans falling from the cupboard can still put a nasty hole in work surface.

  Holes can be repaired – there are even companies that can perform marvellous repairs where they match the pattern of the work surface. But no repairs come cheap.

- **Random Stickers** /Reflectors – Pay attention to seemingly random stickers or reflectors placed on the outside of the caravan. They are often used to cover up damage.

  In all, there are endless things you could check when viewing a caravan. I should know, I wrote a list of 100 of them on my website (you download the check list here www.how2caravan. com/100).

  My advice is to check as much as you can in the given time. If at all possible, take a caravanner along with you, two pairs of eyes are better than one.

CHAPTER 11

Making The Purchase

Let us assume that you have now found "the one", *the* caravan that you are going to buy – all that's left to do now is buy it! But wait... you want to make sure you get the best possible deal you can, right?

There is an art to negotiating a good deal, the best ones are where both parties, buyer and seller come together on the mutual ground. The mutual ground is the agreement on price when no single party feels they got the better end of the bargain.

How To Negotiate A Good Deal Buying From A Dealership

If you decide to buy a caravan from a dealership there are a few tactics that you could employ that will help you to negotiate the best possible deal. Please note that I am not saying that you *should* do all or *any* of these things, some won't suit you or your circumstances. These are just some things you *could* do.

Dealerships enjoy simple transactions that happen quickly and enable them to realise their profits as soon as possible. As a buyer you can leverage that; here are few things to consider:

- Don't trade anything in. If you have a trade in, sell it separately. That way, you get a better price for your trade in and the dealership doesn't have to worry about selling your trade in before they get all of their money.

- Be as flexible as you can. At peak times, your flexibility on collection dates will be greatly appreciated.

- Take the caravan as it is. I understand this comes with its risks, and could be defeat the whole object of buying from a dealership in the first place, but hear me out.

If you are willing to buy the caravan as you see it without the need for it to go through the workshop, be cleaned and come with a warranty then you might be looking at a significant discount.

Not all dealerships would be willing to sell you a caravan this way, and that's fine. But if they are it could help you to get the price down. I would only do this under the following circumstances; I could prove that the caravan had recently had a service, I could see all of the appliances functioning, that there were no obvious signs of damp (realised after my own damp test was carried out) and finally that I was comfortable with and fully understood what I was doing.

- Be nice. This might seem trivial, but it goes a long way. It shouldn't make a difference, but it does. Being rude and nasty to the salesperson is not going to make them want to give you a generous deal.

- Show them you mean business. Don't talk about buying until you are truly ready to buy. A sales person is far less likely to let someone walk away without buying when they are clearly ready to pay a deposit there and then if the deal is right.

- Have your funds ready and available. If a salesperson knows that you are in a position to move forward with the purchase immediately without having to seek funding it can help to speed things up.

- Offer to pay in full at the point of purchase. The dealership may be inclined to offer you a discount if you are willing to pay in full on agreeing the deal, rather than paying a deposit and clearing the final balance on collection day.

- Accept discount in the form of added extras and or accessories. You could save additional costs by getting things thrown in with the deal. This is often preferred by dealers as opposed to giving money off.

Just remember that dealerships are businesses, they need to make profit to pay their staff and their bills, and to continue to offer you support after the purchase. So don't get too upset if they cannot offer you the deal you hoped for.

How To Negotiate A Good Deal Buying Privately

Private sellers are similarly interested in arranging a sale as soon as possible. Here are a few tactics that could help you to negotiate a good deal buying privately:

- Take the money to purchase the caravan with you when you go to view. Nothing says "I am ready to buy" like waving some money in someone's face. Even if it means taking less than they intended, a private seller might just grab the bull by the horns and accept a lower offer.

- Don't complicate things. Be ready to take the caravan there and then. Asking the seller if they could hold onto it for a week or two so you can sort out storage won't help the deal.

- Be nice. Yup, it works privately too. It is likely that you will be viewing the caravan at someone's home. Respect their home and their wishes while you are on their property.

How To Secure The Best Trade In Price

If you have something to trade in, be it another caravan, car, motorhome, motorcycle, etc, you will want to secure the best possible trade in price. Here are a few tips that can help to do just that:

- Ensure you have all the information that the dealership might need to know in order to value it. I'm talking; mileage, recent service work, engine size, etc. Literally give them all the information you have about it.

- Physically take the part exchange to the dealership. This way, the sales person can get a good look at your trade in before a price is offered. If it is not possible to take it, take detailed pictures instead.

- Clean it thoroughly inside and out. The impression that a clean, fresh smelling caravan gives is much better than a dirty, smelly one.

- Be honest about the condition. Bring any damage or known faults to the sales person attention. Honesty goes a long way.

- Don't trade it in, sell it separately. I already talked about this, but it is a solid way to get more money for it.

Make The Most Of The Experts On Hand

Regardless of whether you are buying privately or from a dealership, you have an expert / experts on hand who can tell you everything you need to know. There is nothing worse than owning a caravan, but not having a clue how to use it.

Most dealerships will take you through their handover procedure where they will tell you what everything is and how it works. This is also your opportunity to ask them any questions you might have about the workings of the caravan.

Similarly, a private seller will probably know exactly how everything in their caravan works. Be sure to ask them all you need to know before parting ways.

Closing Out

That's me about done now folks. Thank you again for buying my book – I hope you found it useful and that you can take something from it to help you with your caravan purchase.

I would really appreciate it if you could take the time to write a brief review of the book – you can do so Amazon. It means the world to me to hear what my readers think of my material, even when they don't have anything nice to say. If you can spare two minutes I would really appreciate it:

1. Go to www.amazon.co.uk

2. Search for my book "Confidential Caravan Buying Guide"

3. Click the "Write a customer review" button

4. Let everyone know what you thought about the book

Where Can I Get More Caravanning Advice?

"You mean there's more?" (Horrified face). Oh yes, there is plenty more. I am sure you will still have loads of unanswered questions and maybe even more than you had to before you read the book. It is often the case that in order to answer a question, you must create another. I am here and happy to help you - if I don't know the answer then I'll know where to look to get it. Feel free to email me at Paul@how2caravan.com

Here are some friendly forums I frequent – there are lots of helpful people that will be more than happy to help a fellow caravanner out:

• Caravan Talk

• Caravan Times Community

• Caravan Chat

- The Caravan Channel Forum

There is also a wealth of caravan related advice and information on my blog which you can find at www.how2caravan. com

Printed in Great Britain
by Amazon

78935607R00054